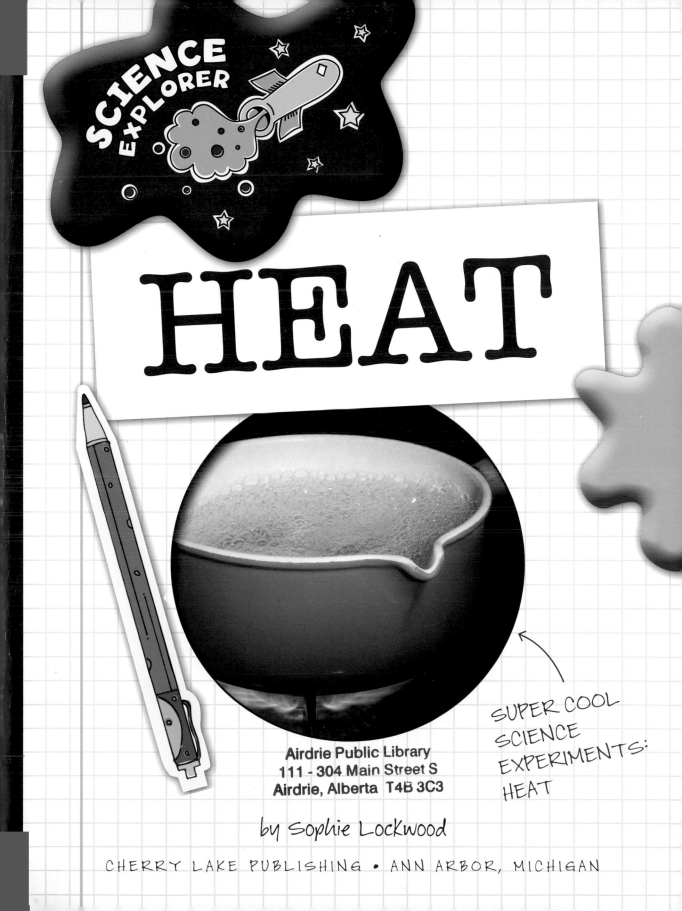

SCIENCE EXPLORER

HEAT

SUPER COOL
SCIENCE
EXPERIMENTS:
HEAT

by Sophie Lockwood

CHERRY LAKE PUBLISHING • ANN ARBOR, MICHIGAN

CHERRY
LAKE
Publishing

Published in the United States of America by
Cherry Lake Publishing
Ann Arbor, Michigan
www.cherrylakepublishing.com

Content Editor: Robert Wolffe, EdD,
Professor of Teacher Education,
Bradley University, Peoria, Illinois

Book design and illustration: The Design Lab

Photo Credits: Cover and pages 1, 8, and 9 ©Kelpfish/Dreamstime.com; page 13, ©Wernersl/Dreamstime.com; page 17, ©Jim West/Alamy; page 18, ©Paul Glendell/Alamy; page 21, ©JUPITERIMAGES/Brand X/Alamy; page 22, ©Adpower99/Dreamstime.com; page 25, ©Kentoh/Dreamstime.com; page 28, ©Blackcheap/Dreamstime.com

Library of Congress Cataloging-in-Publication Data
Lockwood, Sophie.
  Super cool science experiments: heat / by Sophie Lockwood.
     p. cm.—(Science explorer)
  Includes bibliographical references and index.
  ISBN-13: 978-1-60279-534-1   ISBN-10: 1-60279-534-7 (lib. bdg.)
  ISBN-13: 978-1-60279-613-3   ISBN-10: 1-60279-613-0 (pbk.)
 1. Heat—Juvenile literature. I. Title. II. Series.
  QC256.L63 2010
  536—dc22   2009001164

Cherry Lake Publishing would like to acknowledge the work of The Partnership for 21st Century Skills. Please visit www.21stcenturyskills.org for more information.

SCIENCE EXPLORER

HEAT

TABLE OF CONTENTS

Science Is Hot Stuff!

A sweater keeps you warm. A stove heats a pot of soup. Crayons melt in the summer sun. Heat makes changes in your comfort, your food, and things you own. Understanding how heat works is science.

Science affects your life every day. It is all around you. When you investigate how or why things work, you become a scientist. In this book, we'll see how to do real scientific experiments using things you have in your home. We'll do experiments with heat, and we'll do them using the scientific method. You'll make many discoveries along the way!

First Things First

Scientists are curious. They have lots of questions about the things they see around them. They ask questions and do experiments to find answers to those questions. They observe what happens during the experiment. Then they draw conclusions about what they saw.

The first "scientists" to experiment with heat probably lived in caves. Maybe a wildfire passed by, and these prehistoric people found animals killed in the fire. They could not throw away food, but the meat was different from the raw flesh humans normally ate. It was tasty. What changed the meat? How could they make this cooked meat?

They experimented with fire, heated stones, and cooked in pottery jars. They learned how to cook. Cooking is very scientific.

When today's scientists do experiments, they plan all parts of their work. They record their observations. They write notes about what they see and what they learn. But scientists don't rely on just their vision to learn about something. How does something feel? How does it smell? They make observations using all of their senses.

Scientists carefully record their observations.

When scientists design experiments, they must think very clearly. The way they think about problems is often called the scientific method. It's a step-by-step way of finding answers to specific questions. The steps don't always follow the same pattern. Sometimes scientists change their minds. The process often works something like this:

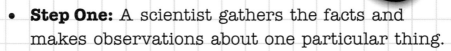

- **Step One:** A scientist gathers the facts and makes observations about one particular thing.
- **Step Two:** The scientist comes up with a question that is not answered by all the observations and facts.
- **Step Three:** The scientist creates a hypothesis. This is a statement of what the scientist thinks is probably the answer to the question.
- **Step Four:** The scientist tests the hypothesis. He or she designs an experiment to see whether the hypothesis is correct. The scientist does the experiment and writes down what happens.
- **Step Five:** The scientist draws a conclusion based on how the experiment turned out. The conclusion might be that the hypothesis is correct. Sometimes, though, the hypothesis is not correct. In that case, the scientist might develop a new hypothesis and another experiment.

My hypothesis was right!

In the following experiments, you'll use the scientific method to do experiments involving heat. You'll plan an experiment based on a question that needs answering. You'll develop a hypothesis that predicts the result of the experiment. Then you'll do an actual experiment to see if the hypothesis was correct. You are the scientist. Are you ready?

Follow the method and you can be a scientist, too!

Experiment #1
Heat It Up!

Caution! Hot stuff!

This is how to start your first experiment. Do some brainstorming. What do you already know about heat? The sun provides heat, and so do radiators, stoves, lightbulbs, and your body. Some materials change when they are heated. What else do you want to know? What substances react to heat? How do they change? What happens when the heat is taken away?

Let's run an experiment that tests what happens when a substance is heated and then allowed to cool. We'll use four substances: chocolate, a crayon, ice, and sugar. Let's form a hypothesis: **When substances are heated, any change that takes place is permanent.** Let's test the hypothesis.

Here's what you'll need:
- 4 pieces of aluminum foil, 3 inches by 3 inches (7.6 centimeters by 7.6 cm)
- A piece of chocolate (unwrapped)
- A crayon (unwrapped)
- An ice cube
- A teaspoonful of sugar
- A heat source, which in this experiment is a desk lamp with a flexible arm
- A timer

Collect the items for this experiment.

10

Instructions:

1. Make four heat pans from the aluminum foil by folding the sides up by 0.4 inch (1 cm). Then pinch the corners. The pans should look like boxes without tops.
2. Put the chocolate in box 1, a crayon in box 2, an ice cube in box 3, and the sugar in box 4.
3. Put box 1 under your heat source. Ask an adult to help you adjust the lamp so the lightbulb is 2 inches (5 cm) above the box. Allow the heat from the lightbulb to heat the box for exactly 5 minutes. Wh happens to the chocolate? Write down the result.
4. Remove the pan and put it to the side.
5. Repeat this process with each box, making sure that each substance remains under the lightbulb for exactly 5 minutes.
6. After 1 hour, take a look at each substance again. Record your observations.

What do you think will happen?

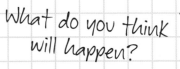

11

Conclusion:

What happened to each substance when it was placed under the heat source for 5 minutes? What happened to the substances after they cooled off? The chocolate and the crayon melted. When they cooled, they returned to solid form. The ice cube melted and became water. The sugar did not change because the lightbulb's heat was not hot enough to melt sugar.

So, our conclusion is that the changes that happen when something is heated are not always permanent. Was our hypothesis correct? No, but that's okay. Scientists get a lot of things wrong at first. Then they think some more and come up with new hypotheses to test. Using the scientific method to answer questions is a challenging process!

You may have heard people say that it is hot enough outside to fry an egg on the sidewalk. The temperature needed to cook an egg is at least 149 degrees Fahrenheit (65 degrees Celsius). Concrete sidewalks rarely get hot enough to fully cook an egg. But scientists are interested in the ways that outdoor surfaces absorb heat. A research group at Worcester Polytechnic Institute is studying asphalt. Could the heat absorbed by asphalt be used as an energy source? Scientists hope to find a way to use that energy to power buildings.

Experiment #2
The Temperature's Rising

What happens to melted candle wax when it cools?

In Experiment #1, we learned that heat could change substances from solids to liquids. We also learned that these changes are not always permanent. The heat that melted the substances in our experiment came from a direct heat source: the lamp. However, the air around the substances also got hot and transferred heat to the substances. When heat is transferred in this way, it is called indirect heat.

We often use indirect heat while cooking. On the stove top, the heating element heats up a metal pot, and the hot metal transfers the heat to the food. In an oven, the heating element heats the air, and the heated air cooks the food.

To cook food, you put it into containers that allow the even transfer of heat. These containers might be pots, pans, dishes, or plates. Most metal, glass, and ceramic substances are good heat conductors. Let's do an experiment about conducting heat. Let's see which surface conducts heat best. What do you think it will be: metal, plastic, or wood? Here are three possible hypotheses for this experiment:

Hypothesis #1: Metal will conduct heat better than plastic or wood.

Hypothesis #2: Plastic will conduct heat better than metal or wood.

Hypothesis #3: Wood will conduct heat better than metal or plastic.

Choose the hypothesis that you think is correct.

Here's what you'll need:

- Butter or solid vegetable shortening
- 3 small plastic beads
- Metal, plastic, and wooden spoons (1 each)
- A small, heatproof glass bowl
- A pot holder or trivet
- Hot, boiled water

Keep an eye on those beads!

Instructions:

1. Using a small dab of butter or shortening, stick a bead onto the handle of each spoon. Be sure to put the bead as close to the end of the spoon's handle as possible.
2. Put the heatproof glass bowl on the pot holder or trivet.
3. Place the spoons in the bowl so that the handles are above the rim of the bowl.

4. Ask an adult to pour a cup of boiling water into the bowl. It should be enough to just cover the shallow bowls of the spoons.

5. Watch what happens. Which bead drops off first? Why? Did you prove your hypothesis? Be sure to record your results.

Be careful with the boiling water!

Let's apply what you learned in Experiment #2 to your life. Picture three park benches. One is made of metal. One is made of light-colored plastic. One is made of wood. All three benches have been in the hot, summer sun for a few minutes. Which bench would be hottest? Why? A metal bench would be very hot. A plastic bench may be warm. A wooden bench might be just right.

Experiment #3
Keeping It Warm

Sometimes, it is important to allow heat to spread or transfer, as in cooking. Other times, you want to keep heat contained. Materials that contain heat are called insulators. You use insulators all the time. Your winter coat insulates you from cold air. It keeps the warmth from your body near you. Your house has insulation to keep heat from escaping through the roof and walls.

Insulators work by trapping air around the hot substance. The air holds the heat.

Good scientists make detailed notes about their observations.

Quick quiz, no fair peeking at the previous page. Why do houses have insulation in the walls?

This heated air is not able to move away easily from the source of the heat.

But what makes a good insulator? It has to be something that does not conduct heat. It also has to trap air around the hot substance. Let's do an experiment to find out what materials are good insulators. You are going to wrap four coffee cups with different kinds of insulators. Which one do you think will work the best? Think about Experiment #2. Which spoons did not conduct heat well? Does that give you a clue? Let's make a hypothesis: **Insulated cups will keep the water warmer than the cup without insulation. The cup wrapped in plastic will hold the heat best.**

Here's what you'll need:

- A newspaper page
- 5 identical coffee cups
- Cellophane tape
- A piece of aluminum foil, 1.6 inches (4 cm) long
- A small plastic trash bag
- An old cotton sock
- Very hot water
- Scissors
- A timer

You probably have all of these items at home.

Instructions:

1. Fold the newspaper to the height of the coffee cup. Wrap the newspaper around the cup and tape it so it stays in place.
2. Do the same thing with the aluminum foil and the plastic trash bag.
3. Cut the bottom off a sock, and slide the top portion around the fourth cup. If you need to, hold the sock in place with tape.
4. One cup will have no insulation.
5. Pour very hot, but not boiling, water into each cup. Fill each cup to about 1 inch (2.5 cm) from the top. Make sure they all have the same amount of water.
6. Set your timer for 15 minutes. After the time is up, test the water carefully with your finger. Which cup has the coolest water? Which has the hottest water? Was your hypothesis correct? Write down your conclusions.

Is newspaper a good insulator or just a good read?

Can you think of a piece of science equipment that you have in your classroom that would make your observations more accurate? You probably said a thermometer. If you use one, you can record exact temperature readings. Why would this be important?

In the winter, you wear a coat to keep your body warm. You put on boots to keep your feet warm and mittens for your hands. If you aren't wearing these insulators, your body's heat escapes more quickly into the cold air. Based on our experiments, what kinds of materials would make good insulation in a winter coat? What kinds of materials would you not want to wear?

Experiment #4 Full of Hot Air

It will take a lot of hot air to get this balloon airborne.

You probably have seen hot air balloons floating through the sky. They are beautiful to watch and a bit of a mystery. How do they work? The balloon operator has a heater that heats the air inside the balloon. As the air heats up, the balloon expands. As long as the air in the balloon is hotter than the air outside, the balloon will rise.

You have observed that hot air balloons expand and rise in the sky. But what makes the balloon expand? Does heating make the air inside it expand? Does hot air always expand? You can test this idea by running an experiment in your kitchen. Here are some possible hypotheses:

Hypothesis #1: Air does not expand when it is heated.

Hypothesis #2: Air expands when it is heated.

Choose the hypothesis you think is correct.

Here's what you'll need:
- A large balloon
- An empty 2-liter soda bottle, with cap off
- Duct tape
- A bucket
- Very hot water
- A pair of kitchen tongs

Get the hot water last.

Instructions:

1. Put the end of the balloon over the opening of the soda bottle. Seal the balloon to the bottle with duct tape.

2. Put the bucket in the kitchen sink and fill it up with very hot water.

3. Using the tongs, push the bottle into the hot water and hold it there. Be careful! You do not want to burn yourself.

The hot water heats the air inside the bottle. What happens to the balloon? Why? Did you prove your hypothesis?

What happens to your balloon?

Why did the balloon in your experiment expand? Gases expand when they are heated. That is because heat gives the gas molecules more energy to move around. The molecules move around and spread out, or expand. They rose into the balloon because the sides of the plastic bottle don't expand as easily as the rubber of the balloon. The air takes the path of least resistance and expands into the balloon. What does this have to do with hot air balloons? The hotter the air gets and the more it expands, the less dense it becomes. A gas that is less dense will float on top of a gas that is more dense. That is why a hot air balloon always rises as long as the air inside the balloon is hotter than the air outside the balloon.

Experiment #5
More Hot Stuff

Have you ever made a model of a molecule?

There are many types of energy. Heat energy is called thermal energy. Thermal energy is a form of kinetic energy. Scientists know that kinetic energy increases as the surrounding temperature increases. When an object becomes hotter, its molecules move faster. These molecules have more kinetic energy than the molecules in a cooler object.

Do you think that heat affects chemical reactions? That's a good question. Let's design an experiment to answer this question. What do we think the experiment will prove? Let's form a hypothesis: **Heat will make a chemical reaction happen faster.**

Here's what you'll need:
- Masking tape
- 2 clear drinking glasses (use heat-resistant or tempered glasses, which are less likely to break during your experiment)
- A marking pen
- ½ cup cold water
- ½ cup warm water
- A small saucepan
- A clock with a second hand
- 2 effervescent antacid tablets (ask an adult to help you find these)

Do you have everything you need?

Instructions:

1. Place a piece of masking tape on each glass.
2. Use the marking pen to write "cold" on one piece of tape and "hot" on the other.
3. Pour ½ cup cold water into the "cold" glass and put it in the freezer for 5 minutes. You want the water to be very cold, but not frozen.
4. Right before you take the cold water out of the freezer, heat ½ cup warm water in the saucepan. Ask an adult to help you. When the water is very hot, but not boiling, pour the water in the glass labeled "hot."
5. Open the package of effervescent antacid tablets. Put the hot and cold glasses next to each other. At the exact same time, drop one tablet in each glass. Note the time. Watch the tablets carefully. Time how long it takes for the tablets to dissolve. Make notes about the time. Which tablet dissolves faster?

What do you observe?

Experiment #6
Do It Yourself!

Some people think we could heat our homes with heat from the sun. Do you think this is possible? You have already learned that metal works as a good heat conductor. You might also know that the color black absorbs heat, and the color white reflects heat.

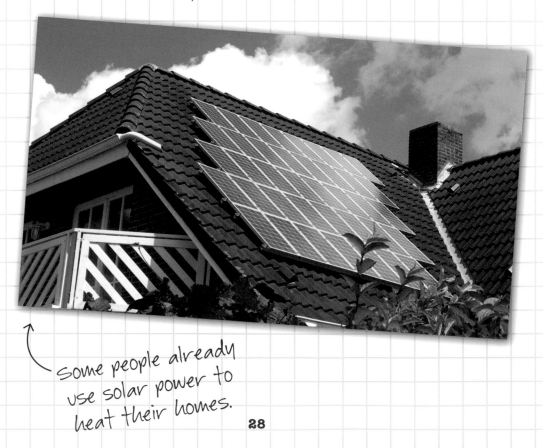

Some people already use solar power to heat their homes.

Use what you know about conductors, insulators, and colors to design an experiment about heating with solar power. First, think about Experiment #1, where you made boxes for heating. You might want to design some type of box for this experiment. How about testing different colored boxes with substances in them and using the sun's heat as your heat source? Write up the list of materials you would use and the instructions. Develop a hypothesis. Then run your experiment and write down your observations.

As a scientist, you can learn new things and have fun. Being a scientist is hot stuff!

Fill these empty boxes with your science ideas!

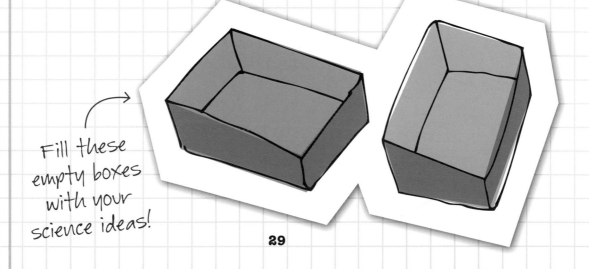

GLOSSARY

chemical reaction (KEM-uh-kuhl ree-AK-shuhn) a process in which two or more substances are changed into one or more new substances

conclusions (kuhn-KLOO-zhuhnz) final decisions, thoughts, or opinions

conductors (kuhn-DUK-terz) substances that allow the transfer of heat or electricity

hypothesis (hy-POTH-uh-sihss) a logical guess about what will happen in an experiment

insulators (IN-suh-lay-terz) materials that slow the loss of heat

kinetic (kih-NET-ik) a form of energy caused by motion

method (METH-uhd) a way of doing something

observations (ob-zur-VAY-shuhnz) things that are seen or noticed with one's senses

solar (SO-luhr) of or from the sun

thermal (THUR-muhl) having to do with heat

transferred (TRANS-ferd) moved or allowed movement from one place to another

FOR MORE INFORMATION

BOOKS

Cook, Trevor. *Experiments with Heat*. New York: PowerKids Press, 2009.

Gardner, Robert. *Temperature and Heat: Great Experiments and Ideas*. Berkeley Heights, NJ: Enslow Publishers, 2009.

WEB SITES

All Science Fair Projects—Heat

www.all-science-fair-projects.com/category58.html

Different projects about heat at the elementary, middle, and high school levels

Exploratorium Science Snacks—Heat

www.exploratorium.edu/snacks/iconheat.html

Ten easy-to-do experiments involving heat

Kid Science Experiments—Heat

www.kids-science-experiments.com/cat_heat.html

A few experiments using heat

INDEX

About the Author

In addition to writing books, Sophie Lockwood does experiments in her kitchen all the time! Although most of the experiments are called dinner, Sophie and her granddaughter actually did every experiment in this book. Sophie lives in South Carolina with her husband and enjoys reading, playing bridge, and watching movies when she isn't writing.